I0158483

I took a quantum leap of faith and fell

I took a
quantum
leap of
faith
and
fell

Tina Quartey

GOLDEN DRAGONFLY PRESS
AMHERST, MASSACHUSETTS
2018

FIRST PRINT EDITION, October 2018
FIRST EBOOK EDITION, October 2018

Sonnet no. 7 was *The American Aesthetic*'s 5th Sonnet Prize Winner and was first published in that journal's Winter 2017–2018 Issue as "A Broken Heart."

ISBN–13: 978–1–7325772–3–7
ISBN–10: 1–7325772–3–4

Library of Congress Control Number: 2018958688

Printed on acid-free paper supplied by a Forest Stewardship Council-certified provider. Cream paper is made from 30% post-consumer waste recycled material.

First published in the United States of America
by Golden Dragonfly Press, 2018.

www.goldendragonflypress.com

In the beginning was desire
And desire was with God
And desire was God

Rig Veda

I

—I—

Remembrance came with you, oh Source of Joy
Your touch forever in my cells ingrained
A dancer who creates and who destroys
Inside me, letting only truth remain
From years of sleep I was blessed to be awakened
And lovingly guided to find my buried lust
Into the core of my being I was shaken
But not afraid, in my unbroken trust
You break the spell of shame and of conventions
My body now remembers how to breathe
My mind is blown and opened to new dimensions
To layers of knowledge and secrets underneath
    Enabled by someone gifted with virtual seeing
    From hereon starts my journey of truly being

The purest well of life you are to me
A stream so crystal clear, a running river
That inundates with sacred ecstasy
My every cell, and makes my body quiver
But after oneness, unity and bliss
The doubt if there is mutual affection
The sadness, longing for an earthly kiss
Replaces feeling of profound connection
With fear I long to hear your truthful voice
Am I a puppet in your world of magic?
For me there was not really any choice
But is my love for you nothing but tragic?
    Invincible this flood I never knew
    Not ever have I loved as I love you

—3—

Do not believe I want to end this pain
With joy, abundance, willingness I'm bleeding
So rip my heart out and cut every vein
And fertilise the soil before the seeding
My naked soul in fearlessness I give
My truthful body, aching from desire
In lies I do not ever want to live
So cleanse me, let me walk into the fire
Inside you, let me die from self, from fear
To born again in love, in truth, in seeing
To wash away the veil with blissful tears
And let shine through the essence of our being
    A glimpse that all is one and one is all
    Into what is, in love, just let me fall

–4–

Somewhere the full moon shines on you this night
Its alchemy the dust to silver turning
But have you ceased to shed on me your light
And left my searching soul in hopeless yearning?
So helplessly I begged you to reply
Humiliated in my deep confusion
Were teachings you once shared simply denied?
Were sacred bonds of trust but an illusion?
I know there is another way to speak
That's wordless, limitless, beyond perception
Beyond the validation that I seek
Beyond the false, the lie and the deception
 And in that realm an insight have I gained
 The giving of oneself can't be reclaimed

(From a dream)
I saw the path that leads to paradise
Beginning at the outskirts of the city
All visible, outlined and undisguised
For those whose eyes had cleared themselves from pity
But as I moved towards that lovely lane
I felt a calling, like a soundless crying
From someone suffering in quiet pain
I shivered, wondered what I'd been denying
When searching through the alleys (for a sign)
I saw a boy, abandoned in the shadows
It broke my heart; I knew that he was mine
And he had never played on sunny meadows
    How beckoning the road to Eden winds
    But Inner Child may not be left behind

He kneels down in the dirt to warm the ground
The soil is frozen where she grows, this flower
The bud's uptight and cold, but when she's found
The sun's reflected in the palms that hold her
In this man's hands she dares herself to lean
(A gardener; his hand's not lost its cunning)
Her petals open, longing to be seen
And when revealed he finds her beauty stunning
But when he looks more closely, she's too wild
Is she some kind of weed? She does look shady…
Needs to be shaped, transformed from flowerchild
To earn her dignity as flowerlady
    In broken beauty; petals on the clay
    Without a word he turns and walks away

I never knew a broken heart could break
And scatter in a squillion broken atoms
That every little atom thus could ache
In brokenness beyond what mind can fathom
I never knew abandoned could be left
To loneliness beyond all lonely longing
That giving of oneself could turn to theft
That violated sense of deep belonging
I never knew that pain's a gift of gold
Vulnerability the path to fullness
That breaking even more can make you whole
And crack those broken atoms into oneness
    So to that golden pain I fully give
    Myself (the only way to fully live)

II

–8–

I lost you, oh Beloved, many times
With every fibre of my being screaming
And t'wards the sky I reached my hands and whined
As earth had rifted and had left no meaning
I lost you in a war with reckless slaughter
The one to whom my soul's forever tied
I lost you as a son and as a daughter
Before my eyes or in my arms you died
And with your deaths I died and died again
Was raped and ripped apart and cut to pieces
And only one thing brutally remained:
The pain that never ends, that never ceases
    And just as deep the wounds so deep the fear
    Of loving, being loved and being near

Nobody ever touched me like you did
Far deeper than the deepest of the oceans
And in the holy water's depth I hid
My innermost desires and emotions
A reconnection, an initiation
A cry of birth that nobody could hear
Inevitably served as invocation
Of childhood wounds and deeply rooted fears
Betrayal was to whom I did confess
Abandonment to whom my soul was reaching
My one true love was only Emptiness
Denial brought me love's abyssal teachings
    But Innocence may never this conceive;
    How you could touch so deeply, then just leave

The cruellest of months, and earth is frozen
But torn inside by hidden lava streams
A wasteland for the ones who were not chosen
In ruins of our shattered, hidden dreams
My limbs are weakened and my pulse is failing
My life force drained as by a parasite
My sight's obscured like looking through a veiling
A lost involuntary eremite
Rejected was my deepest recognition
A fatal sense of souls' affinity
A death's refinement through the demolition
Of self, in my untouchability
    A desolated landscape, raw and bare
    But reckless love persists in empty air

–II–

We are the dancers on the fringe of darkness
The choreography of dominance
Contempt and righteousness expressed with harshness
That breaks my spirit, shames my luminance
A template was ingrained by generations
A deep attraction pulls t'wards that black hole
A wall of fear keeps us in separation
An urge to be controlled or in control
Behind that need to dominate I see
A child that had to hide in Shadowland
Rejected, not allowed to fully be
Himself, and no one there to hold his hand
    Embrace I will that child in reverence
    Protecting with my love his innocence

As Mnemosyne awakes me in the morning
Projecting painful pictures from the past
She firmly puts me into mode of mourning
The torments (and the love that did not last)
In vain I call on Dike to accuse
My perpetrators posing as my saviours
But gas will shed its light upon abuse
And twistedly legitimise behaviours
Descending through the lanes of deep depression
In corridors of death and of defeat
I'm stripped of all my powers and possessions
And hung up on a hook like slaughtered meat
    And everyone's prepared to cloak the violence
    And every cry for help is met with silence

−13−

My Lilith, dressed in black, no light she bears
I want to take that precious silver crescent
To crown her as the Goddess of Despair
With endless cycles in a pain incessant
And when did I lose count of all lunations
I spent in fateful faith inside my cave?
Who beats the drum for me, for my salvation?
(If my devotion should become my grave)
I'm standing on the edge of the abyss
And begging you for cruel honesty
Now make me take the leap, be merciless
That I may walk my path relentlessly
    But even through excruciating deaths
    The sense of you in me with every breath

I am the Knight of Nights, my truth I shine
Upon the shamed, the hidden and the rotten
I am the serpent coiled up in your spine
Disturbs the peace and brings up what's forgotten
I am the mirror that reflects your light
While (to avoid your shadow) you keep running
Escaping pains and wounds in futile fight
While innermost desires you are shunning
I am the hidden child that you reject
Whose faith and trust and innocence were broken
By silent treatment, harshness and neglect
Unheard, ignored or silenced when he'd spoken
    I'm Goddess of Discord, a gift I'm bringing:
    I hear the false notes in the song you're singing

III

−15−

My song's a sword, a ray of blue remembrance
That's cutting through oblivion and lies
It clears the fog, allows for the transcendence
And liberates from old beliefs and ties
So as a warrior my way I fought
Through water, desert and through burning fire
To find you hanging in a tree of thoughts
Alive, but upside down, in twisted wires
Forgotten was our soul's true history
Well buried under fears and deep resistance
But you had shown me true love's mystery
Which set in motion our whole existence
    Whilst you seek safety behind high walls
    The mighty tower, stone by stone, will fall

–16–

With eyes wide open though he's fast asleep
He's riding through the dark night on his quest
His horse is tired and the road is steep
Frostbitten is the rosebud in his chest
In shining armour searching for the source
The well of love, of life, of purity
Not realising inside him flows this force
That power dwells in vulnerability
But will he have the courage to receive
The Grail and drink? as he's afraid to drown
And lose himself, while he does not believe
That death can bring him his awaited crown
    Already shimmering above his head
    While he still clings to what since long is dead

−17−

How much denial can the Goddess take
Before the world is shattered by her grieving?
Your walls are trembling and your ground does shake
In frosty fright resisting, not receiving
Cause love is merciless and all revealing
That in the secret chambers of your heart
Awaits that rage of love, that painful healing
Allowing false control to fall apart
But pain and grace are neighbours, can't you see?
When you allow the softening and purging
Surrendering the »I« embracing »we«
In sacred intimacy through the merging
    And standing in the light of goddess presence
    That wave of love; that is in truth your essence

–18–

I love this spring so merciful and cold
The showering of rainy grace and prayers
Not forcing me too quickly to unfold
Just carefully removing pupa layers
More boldly open flower buds of May
From Mother Nature fearing no rejection
And planted seeds will never feel betrayed
When blessed by Taurus is the earth's conception
In metamorphosis I cannot cling
To old and safe, in fear of getting burned
I have no choice but to stretch out those wings
In faith, beyond the point of no return
    As Venus softly calls me to surrender:
    The blessings from her light, so bright and tender

Every thing is sacred, every moment
When one perceives it all through eyes of love
The smallest most mundane of life components
A miracle, created from above
Thus is my love a gift (though unrequited)
A blessing from the heavens and a sign
That I am his, even if ununited
Unkissed and unembraced, cause he's not mine
I'm Ganga, hidden deep in Shiva's hair
So close, yet so remote, a distant presence
Entangled in devotion and despair
Embedded in his energy, his essence
    With all I am, with everything I do
    With every breath I take I honour you

20

This full moon brings the gift of lilies white
A portal opens to the final merging
In faithfulness »till Death do us unite«
I do allow and welcome what's emerging
And once I stood before you, raw and naked
Prepared to fully enter the unknown
Evoked the irrevocable and sacred
The bond that makes the unknown feel like home
A rite of passage, and I did descend
To own my powerlessness and my power
Surrendered and with nothing to defend
I gave myself, from bud to fading flower
    In willingness those thousand deaths to die
    Then daring to unfold the wings and fly

21

I took a quantum leap of faith and fell
Beatifying blast waves through my being
Did penetrate my core and crack my shell
And opened eyes to unseen ways of seeing
Your touchless touch had made me bodiless
Defrosted and unlocked in fretless falling
Through timelines in the space of emptiness
Where Kamadeva hit me with a calling
Unsynchronized with present time and space
Embodying the deepest of emotions
My love's so innocently out of place
But only deeper grows my pure devotion
    In recognition of a sacredness
    Of God, in your divine, bare humanness

यद्यत्कर्म करोमि तत्तदखिलं शम्भो तवाराधनम्